RiPPLE 2023

Good luck with your future projects. Ross (the Influencer)

you're [amazing?]
SM.

If you're as good an Architect as an artist JJ Clare Tran ♡ you're going to go.

Thank you for your very beautiful work & for! letting the world see it. Keep shining ♡ - loads of love Rakhi

Don't quit [signature]

Roy

Write on! -Ezgi

Love Tal

You're the sweetest, love your style -Sabrina

Write on! Rachel ♡

All the best Saida

Best of luck in the future - Steve Kent

RiPPLE
2023

A Kingston University Student **Anthology**

19th Edition

Text copyright © the individual athors.

Photographs / artwork copyright © the individual creators.

The moral rights of the authors have been asserted.

First published in 2023 by Kingston University Press.

All rights reserved. No part of this publication may be reproduced or transmitted, in any form or by any means electronic or mechanical, including photocopy, recording, or any information storage and retrieval system, without prior permission of the publisher.

These stories are works of fiction.

Any resemblance to real person living
or dead is purely coincidental.

A catalogue of this book is available from the British Library

ISBN 978 1 909362 75 8

Typeset in Bell MT, Arial, Beloved Ornaments, Hiragino Sans GB, Acumin Variable Concept, Baskerville

Editorial and Design by: Kieran Athayde, Lucy Ashworth, Senait Wondu Mekonnen and Patricia Mercado.

KINGSTON UNIVERSITY PRESS
Kingston University
Penrhyn Road
Kingston-upon-Thames
KT1 2EE

www.kingstonripple.wordpress.com
Instagram account: @ripple_kingston

RiPPLE TEAM '23

Managing Editor
Rakhi Kohli

Design
Heidi Andreassen
Tal Rejwan
Lily Jones
Tara Hiralal
Felix Orlo

Marketing
Tal Rejwan
Ezgi Gürhan
Ekene Ugbaja
Lily Jones
Saida Adila
Hannah Olesen
Marissa Sanchez
Arty Prakasen

Editing
Caitlin Morgan
Mekhla Paul
Hannah Olesen
Heidi Andreassen
Ezgi Gürhan
Tal Rejwan
Rachel Matthews
Rakshita Pawar
Hellia Esat
Farah Nadia
Saida Adila
Manukriti
Maja Kristiansen

Tech
Caitlin Morgan
Heidi Andreassen
Rachel Matthews

Saida Adila
Xyvah M. Okoye

Judging

Tara Hiralal
Caitlin Morgan
Manukriti
Farah Nadia
Yiran Wei
Ezgi Gürhan
Tal Rejwan
Ekene Ugbaja
Rachel Matthews
Rakshita Pawar
Hellia Esat
Marissa Sanchez
Mekhla Paul

Social Media

Lily Jones
Marissa Sanchez
Tara Hiralal
Yiran Wei
Heidi Andreassen
Rachel Matthews

Podcast

Ezgi Gürhan
Tal Rejwan
Rachel Matthews
Ekene Ugbaja
Hannah Olesen
Maja Kristiansen

CONTENTS

Acknowledgements	xii
Prose	1
The Mermaid Joshua Ciccone	2
You and the House Kathleen Fairweather	8
Artwork: Through the Door Zeynep Zee Sertkaya	13
The Art of Silent Communication Rakhi Kohli	14
Poems	17
Celestial Lillian Cowdery	18
A Raindrop Jad H. Al Shara'a	20
Photograph Shreyash Pant	21

Artwork: The Pursuit	22
Greta Jonas	
Sometimes ...	23
Mekhla Paul	
A Collection of Haikus	24
Saida Adila binti Sukman	
Silence is Power	26
Ezgi Gürhan	
Being a Woman	28
Margaret Schnekenburger	
Growth	30
Patricia Mercado	
bus stop	32
Felix Orlo	
Ripples in the Pond	34
Jade Marney	
Artwork: Innocence	35
Tal Rejwan	
Photograph	36
Ellen Warner	
Violence	38
Leah Armstrong	
Peace	39
Lillian Cowdery	
Short Stories	41

The Memory Shop — 42
Rachel Matthews

Tall and Quiet and Almost Nothing — 51
Reuben John Loftus

Artwork: I see the colour — 54
Melissa Benfalami

Artwork: You don't own me — 55
Melissa Benfalami

English↔Chinese Romantic Dictionary (Excerpt\English Version) — 56
Yiran Wei

Amy's Ending — 58
Heidi Andreassen

Artwork: The Weight of the Crown — 60
Lucius Strauss

The Influencer — 61
Ross Sullivan

Sunk-Cost Fallacy — 69
Julia Jacqueline Clara Tracey

A Ghost Story — 73
Chloë Bell

Artwork: U got the Look — 76
Luca Serra

Artwork: Watercolour & Braid Fits — 77
Luca Serra

The Dead Were Never From Florida — 78
Xyvah M. Okoye

Where it Cuts Deep	84
Rachel Matthews	
Legs in Butter	91
Deborah Thompson	
Crow, Devil, God	94
Phoebe Levins	
Artwork: Two Horns	100
Saleha Bakhtiar	
Grief	101
Ruairidh MacLean	
This Year's Creatives	104
About Kingston University Press	114

Acknowledgements

During the 19 years of RiPPLE's existence, it has strived to give voice to the myriad of students at Kingston University. Despite the continuous academic pressures plaguing the students, RiPPLE has always provided creative respite, acceptance, and a platform to voice any thought without judgement.

When we first started the journey of producing the 2023 edition of RiPPLE, it seemed like we were trying to look for a summit high up in the clouds, and that the climb to get there would be a long and daunting journey. Yet here we are, already wrapping up the 2023 edition. The time flew and the journey became a fun hike with my team.

It goes without saying that this would not have been possible without the unparalleled support, hard work and dedication of this year's team. All of them have been invaluable pillars and to singularly list all the contributions would take over this book. From hosting workshops, editing, re-editing, handing out flyers, recording podcasts, and to getting the greatest number of submissions in RiPPLE history! We have done it all together and I could not be prouder.

But I would like to extend my sincerest appreciation towards my head of social media and marketing—Felix Orlo. She has been the bearer of my confidences, my extended creative limb when I did not have one of my own, and a marketing wizard.

I could not have done this without you and our Tuesday lunch sessions. I would also like to thank Emma Tait, course leader of MA Publishing and Kingston University Press Publisher. Thank you for having faith in me with this project and sharing your illimitable practical knowledge of the industry. It has been pivotal to this project.

Naturally, this book would not be possible without the sublime talent of the Kingston University students who sent us their work. It was a privilege to be able to publish all the different mediums of expression we received — paintings, graphic designs, poems, short stories, letters of love and so much more. I am proud to be part of this journey to publish exemplary works of students that continue to push creative boundaries. I wish all contributors the best for their future and hope to see more of their published works.

Lastly, I would like to thank you dear reader for picking up this book and being a part of our journey to the summit. I know the view at the top will astound you as much as it has astounded our team.

Rakhi Kohli
Managing Editor, RiPPLE 2023

"Always be a poet, even in prose."

— *Charles Baudelaire*

The Mermaid

Joshua Ciccone

Water.
 Air.
Struggling legs.

She swam, thrashed, fought towards the surface, kicking her new legs under her, mouth agape and salty brine rushing down her throat and into her lungs. Her arms were strong, but her legs were far, far less than that. They were shrivelled, old, barely usable. New, but dead. Lifeless.

And so was she, for the surface was far too many centimetres, miles, leagues away for her to get to.

Her fair, beautiful skin shimmered as the sun beat down through the water. She gagged, coughed and went still. The last droplets of air escaped her lips. Somewhere far, far below, a deep laugh sounded out through the waters.

They found her body some days after, already turned blue from the lack of air. Her eyes bugged out of her skull and her tongue lolled out of shrivelled lips. Her cheekbones stuck out horribly, and her hair was strung out all over her face and neck.

It was her legs that were the cause of much speculation. The skin on them were so dead that they had turned a muddy brown, and what should have been bones felt more like a sack of jumbled rocks in a leather bag.

There was some whispering about the legs: some of the men said it looked like a fish; that the woman's legs were scaled, not rotten. But they could not come to a solid conclusion and so the conversation stopped.

She was caught in a fish trap and was only discovered after they had taken things to shore. A hard *thump* was heard by most men on the boat as the body tumbled out with the fish, and the skipper let out a yelp loud enough to get most of the crew running to him.

The body smelled of salt and fish and something else, something far more toxic. The mixture made it acidic the closer you got, made your eyes water, made tears tumble down your cheeks and your chin and your neck.

'Does anyone know who she is? Anyone recognise her?' the captain coughed.

A row of fishermen with shaking heads, tears all in their eyes. One of them sniffled.

'Well. Let's clean this up then.'

A burial seemed to be the only thing they could give. The captain carried the body to the shore and they took their shovels and started to dig. And when they were done, they stood around the hole and they held their hats to their chests.

"Well," the captain mumbled, "I'll say a few words, then."

The mumbled words could barely be heard by the other fishermen, but the embarrassment was saved by a soft cough from behind them. They turned.

He was a fair, soft-haired, ridiculously handsome man, with skin that gleamed and a frame that could only be ogled at. His teeth weren't white, but they were close enough that it was somehow more impressive. He oozed charm. He almost shone with his bright clothes and clean skin. His posture was good and his stance was slouched, relaxed and disarming.

'My Prince!' All men averted their eyes.

'What's this here?' the Prince said, his words dripping with honey.

Some more mumbling and shuffling of feet.

The Prince took a step forward and looked into the pit. His eyes were already filled with tears from that acidic salty smell that plagued their eyes. The fishermen stepped back, eyes averted, some shaking from the fear that this man—the Prince!—would accuse them of killing this woman.

But that accusation never came. The Prince took a step and hunched down, climbing down into the hole and lifted up the woman's body.

Later the fishermen would deny that they had ever been there. But most would remember the look that slid over the Prince's face: the awed, hungry, lusty look that shimmered over his fine features as he picked up the woman's body and stared deep into her eyes.

He saw Her first on the beach. A stunning creature, so smooth and bright and shimmering. He wasn't… entirely sure what he had been doing before he came across Her. Why had he been at the beach? It was not his normal haunt—that would be the local tavern, or the barracks of the palace.

He remembered seeing those men… fishermen?… and he remembered climbing into a hole that they had dug into the beach, where She was.

And he remembered looking into Her eyes.

He remembered suddenly feeling very lost.

And then that feeling was replaced by something far stronger. What was it? Love? Lust? All sorts of feelings were rushing through him, mushing together in his stomach into a soup of throbbing, angry, horny feeling that felt near to bubbling over his throat and through his teeth.

He remembered picking up the limp, beautiful body of the woman. That was when that word crawled to the front of his mind: Mermaid.

He had heard of the creatures that lived not two miles off the coast of his country. Who hadn't heard the stories…

stories of women sitting on stones miles away from the coast, stories of things caught in traps that looked almost human, that escaped. You heard stories…

But he didn't think of those stories when he saw Her. What he thought was: *I need Her.*

And have Her he did. He kept the body close, wrapping his arms so tight around Her that his hands almost connected around his back. His legs were shaky, almost completely gone by the time he had stepped out of the hole in the sand.

The fishermen were gone. He wasn't sure how long he had been standing there. Water had pooled into the hole, going up to his knees. The water was cold, numbing and freezing to stand in.

He walked. He drank in Her scent. And then he walked some more.

Soon he forgot how he had found Her. All he needed was to hold her and to walk, though where he was walking to, he wasn't sure.

It was no matter.

The sun was starting to set. The sea was coming in. The beach was empty.

He turned and he walked into the sea. The water lapped around his ankles, his calves and then his knees and hips.

There was a moment of crystal clarity as the water went over his mouth and nose. *What am I doing?* The thought clattered around his head, getting smaller and smaller as he walked.

And the thought dissipated as his breath escaped his lungs

and he sank deeper into the sea. His eyes closed, his muscles locked, and his life started to escape him.

The Prince's last thought wasn't a coherent one; more of an intense feeling of fear, confusion and pain.

But soon none of those feelings were in his hard, dead body. And that laugh, the one that reverberated through the whole ocean, could be heard again.

There were a few days of worry when they could not find the Prince. When his body washed to the shore, it took them a few more to identify him. There were months, years, decades of talk as they tried to discover what had happened.

There were stories, too, of the Prince's legs. They said that they had been found rotten, blackened, almost scaly in their look. They said he almost looked like a fish when they found him: a fish with the body of a human from the waist up. Like a merman, some said.

Most didn't speak of the legs at all. They kept it in their minds instead and they looked at the ocean with trepidation.

You and the House

Kathleen Fairweather

This house is of madness. You've known it since you were small.

In turn, it has known your madness since you were small. You grew up in the house and the house grew up around you. You have the same memories and the same diseases. It remembers your first steps and your first scrapes and your first mistakes. You have grown together, entwined in the same sickness that reeks of nettles and burning and everything mundane yet poisonous.

This house is of your family, your kin. It is your father, fickle and bull-necked with a voice that could crack china. It is his jovial selfish jokes, the only bit of tenderness you could seek from him. Most of all, it is his slamming of the door, reverberating through your latticework spine and steel-pipe soul.

It is your mother, pale and grinning and constantly trotting up and down and across the landing. It is her laugh, shattering like loosely held champagne glasses against your hardwood nerves. It is the crook of the cigarette in her finger, almost beckoning you. Most of all, it is her strands of fine bone-colour hair you find strewn across the place, in the crevices of chairs, even now.

It is your brothers, one big and one little. The world pulled the big one away, death taking him even faster than it did your mother's mother and your father's father. The little one is alive, but just as gone. It is their silhouettes framed in the doorway, their smiles that could both enrage or enrich you, their boots scuffed with mud. It is your big brother's journals that chronicled each day with frenetic scribbles and the ugly drawing he did of you while you were watching from the foot of the bed. It is your little brother's light dancing feet, taking the stairs two-at-a-time and kicking against yours at the dinner table. Most of all, it is knowing the demonstrable feeling of allyship with a touch of enmity and knowing that it cannot last.

It is the cat and dog buried in the yard. The cat with hackles raised and ears pulled back, spitting and scratching at the gaping maw of the attic with blunt claws. Torn apart by a fox, left on the doorstep like the cat would leave shrews. The dog, patient and sniffing and desperate for love where there was none to be found. It gives birth on your bed as you sleep until your ivory sheets are slick with blood. It is squirming puppies shoved in a sack and tossed in the deep winter-river beyond the trees on the horizon before they could open their eyes. It is you screaming on behalf of the dog, who could not, and who died on your bed as you slept. Most of all, it is their skeletons, feeding the earthy roots of the house, more than they ever could when they were breathing and warm.

It is the independent parts of that great seething mass you all called home. It is what grew and bloomed and festered when the rest of you weren't watching. It is the screech of flowery branches, clawing at the windowpane in agonising reproach while your father hacked at its base, his sweat dripping into the dirt. It is the mould that grew behind your mother's closet that left her bedridden for months, bloodstained tissues sucking what was left of the colour in her cheeks. It is the grand piano's strings snapping, sounding like a gunshot as you and your brothers run your still-small hands over the untuned keys, turning your little brother's tears of laughter into tears of fright. It is in the shadows, where you swear you see things, but no one believes you. In the attic, golden glaring slits of eyes challenge you from across the room as you try to capture moths fleeing from the darkness. In the basement, the hum of the boiler becomes the whine of a great slavering beast. In the shed at the end of the yard, you see murky outlines of slender figures and light from a bulb that is broken. Most of all, it is the untameable stretch of land behind the house, the yard, that has never bent to your father's whims of landscaping or your mother's fancies of gardening. Always edging closer to the porch, that veritable jungle of tall grass and weeds, where more than once you and your brothers slunk back stinging and sore.

It is you (most of all, it is you). You are the concierge of yourself and everything you have ever been. You are the boatswain of this great ship now, caretaker of your casket. You and this house are one and the same.

This house is weak and frail, rocking on its haunches unsteadily. From birth you have been a sickly child, lungs rattling with each shaky breath.

This house is vicious and cruel. It thrives on blood spilt, and the industrial-grade cleaner under the kitchen sink. Kindness has never come easily to you either.

This house is pockmarked - cratered with acrid hatred of itself. You look in the mirror when you are thirteen and wish to take a needle and poke-pierce the imperfections out of your face.

This house slices at you like the good knives in the cutlery drawer, the ones you set on the good tablecloth for when good people come to visit. Not like the people in the house. You know that too—rarely does the house make room for good people.

This house is silent and solitary and selfish. It stretches up to the sky as if in some competition, yet it is alone in that too. You hardly speak to anyone anymore.

A list of things the house is not, that it could never touch; your father's mother, quiet yet kind, who never stepped over the property boundary and who you haven't seen since you were small; the squirrels on the edge of the garden, wary and precious, the freshly fallen snow, incorruptible by the tar-black shingles or the venom-yellow gras; the dandelion seeds, who could always escape with one gust of wind.

You hate this house. This house hates you too. You still cut yourself on its sharp edges—the creaks in the stairwell, the nicks in the wallpaper, the dust on the framed photos. You can't bear to touch any of it and you know that the house finds this funny. It is unforgiving in its emptiness, in its desolation. It does not forgive you specifically.

You do not forgive yourself.

Through the Door

Zeynep Zee Sertkaya

The Art of Silent Communication

Rakhi Kohli

They sat unspeaking across from each other in the crowded restaurant, their gaze not breaking. Reality loomed outside the dinner place, they wished nothing more than to delay the inevitable. For it was waiting for them outside the hexagonal walls of the sushi bar. Reality, that this would be the last time they see each other. Neither of them was ready to escape their own fictional world on that tiny four-by-four table for two. But she had a flight to catch and he a bus back home. As they left, hand in hand to their respective ultimate destinations, no words were spoken. Only spasms of interlocked fingers: a reminder that they were still there. They communicated in silence, for all that needed to be said was already understood. They parted ways at the T, one final kiss: a reminder for what awaits till the next time, if there was a next time. She took the descending stairs to the tube station. He opened the door to his taxi. Their eyes already on each other as they both turned for one last look. Their eyes communicating what could not be said in words. She raised the small of her hand to wave goodbye reluctantly. He mirrored her, in action and in emotion, as they took a deep breath, gathered their courage and left. Full, yet broken hearts in tow.

"Poetry is a deal of joy and pain and wonder, with a dash of the dictionary."

— *Khalil Gibran*

Celestial

Lillian Cowdery

Trapped underwater,
Yet still breathing densely sliced air,
Hands running through my hair,
Trying to pull me out.
I bite my tongue,
Drawing blood from unsaid words,
My knees hit a dark, cold, stoned floor,
Speckles of gold reflecting into the mirrors surrounding me.
No way out but to go within.

My skin burns from the stares of so many,
Ears weep from the voices deep inside.
I stare at the creature before me,
Her sly grin mocking my bruises.
Yet when I look further,
I feel her pitiful gaze upon me,
And realise that she is not a monster at all.

Her glowing hands reach for me,
Ethereal golden hair flowing behind her,
Like the river she mustahave drifted in,
Or the celestial skies she fell from,
For she fell too,
Just as I had,
As we all have.
But falling was no limitation,
As she gripped my cold hands,
And picked me up from the pool of crimson.
I walked to the looking glass,
She smiled,
And I smiled too.

A Raindrop

Jad H. Al Shara'a

A raindrop trembling by the window's pane
    Eager and fragile like a dreamful swain
In it reflects his moony night
    And his pensive sight
For what is his smile worth
    In the absence of its easeful warmth
Or what he is set to achieve
    On his lonely night eve
In his reflection he sees days gone by
    In his boundless starry sky
And in its imminent fall he feels
    What he most cowardly fears
The night when he calls you his
    For his love can no longer be a dream

Shreyash Pant

> I wandered
> In the dark, in the silence
> To keep the fresh memory
> dead
> Tired of wishes,
> Empty of dreams
> hungry for joy
> I stood silent
> full of thoughts
> and said to myself
> with a voice like Dust
> tell me
> what is happiness?

The Pursuit

Greta Jonas

Sometimes ...
Mekhla Paul

Sometimes it is just easier to erase someone completely,
Rather than just hanging onto the almost broken thread that
holds you & them.
Sometimes it is just easier to erase someone completely,
Rather than just holding onto the now almost faded memories.
Sometimes it is just easier to erase someone completely,
Rather than waiting for their implausible return.
Sometimes it is just easier to erase someone completely,
Rather than being the one who always hopes for
just another chance.

A Collection of Haikus

Saida Adila binti Sukman

destroy

on a gloomy day
illusions of forever
destroyed in seconds

broken

i think you broke me
shattered my heart, made me cry
but still i love you

winter

once upon a time
before winter turns to spring
my heart beats for you

eyes

a smile crossed his face
scents of blossoms filled the air
there's love in his eyes

                                                summer

                                  coffee and croissants
                    sweet smell in the summer's heat
                                    your soft lips on mine

warmth

the leaves are falling
as I sat there watching him
his smile warms my heart

                                              happiness

                                when the last snow melts
                        at our special place, we dream
                                  of that happiness

Silence is Power

Ezgi Gürhan

Turn the other cheek
Don't strike back

True strength is within
Let your soul waste away

Being hurt isn't so bad
Better you than them

People are precious
Important and fragile

Be strong
Laugh it off

Why so offended
Only words and blows

They only called you
A fool, an idiot
Hit and pushed
It'll heal
Why make
A big deal

It'll only hurt others
It's better you than them.

Being a Woman

Margaret Schnekenburger

To be a presenting woman is to be born with innate fear
And embedded inferiority
To be a woman is to carry a weight you may choose to be ignorant about
But once you acknowledge its presence
It is not something that can be wilfully ignored
To be a woman is to be afraid
Afraid that what was unwillingly given to me biologically
Will ultimately be weaponized against me
My own body shall be the sword that cuts me daily

                                         Am I being too negative?

I do not care
To be a woman is to wish to be a man
Not physically, or literally, but socially
I wish to walk the woods alone at night
I wish to not feel the obligation to hide my body in public
Since it has been so commercialized and objectified
I wish to travel the world safely alone
I wish to be free from the shackles of my sex
Do not misunderstand me —
I love women and the beauty of femininity
But its burden is so hard to bear

                                      When will we be liberated?

Growth

Patricia Mercado

I wonder where I lost myself,
Was it that time when I was sixteen inside
a therapist's office,
where more roads diverged, rather than connected.
Where I faked a smile because I didn't want
my truths to be discovered or,
could it be when you let go of my hand
on that cold night in November.
When you taught me that sometimes
you aren't enough for someone
and that has stuck with me ever since.

Maybe I got lost chasing a new version of me,
one that is no longer intertwined with you.
Yet I only find myself going in circles,
moving like Pan chasing after his lost shadow,
versions of me that I have long since outgrown.
And over and over again I feel,

s-u-f-f-o-c-a-t-e-d.
I can no longer look at my reflection without seeing
20 different faces, like staring into a broken
mirror, fragmented and cracked.
Perhaps you'll find me everywhere,
in my favourite café, between the pages of a book,
the cup I always used in your house,
between those sheets or that Japanese restaurant.

But it is many things, many moments and I
cannot pin-point the exact time, exact causes where I
no longer knew who I was.
But when I am surrounded with friends,
hear the laughter of my family,
sitting on the library floor writing poetry or
inside a church,
I tell myself,
I feel the love you have so selfishly withheld.

bus stop

Felix Orlo

bus stop, bus stop,

gotta get a proper job,
Netflix on my laptop,
wash face, cocopops,
soap operas, shot to shit,

                              you don't get to keep your tips.

hubbabubba, gobstopper,
Happy Shopper, space-hopper,
retail buyer, washer dryer,

                              what the fuck's an air fryer?

emoji pills, oil spills,
Happy Meal, phone bills,
pebble dash, whiplash,

                              sorry love, don't carry cash.

tit-for-tat, bric-a-brac,
cat sick on my rucksack,
nik-naks, pack of quavers,

soles of shoes like alligators,
Aesop's fables, lay a cable,
never check the bus timetable,
scheming soup, suckerpunch,

                         have you rung your mum this month?

good cop, bad cop, bad cop,
bad cop, bad cop—

                         are you happy with your lot?

phone upgrade, tailor made,
hope i'm gonna to be okay,
lost a hoop, vindaloo,
quit my job out of the blue,
damp rot, day light robbed,
don't be dumb, don't get lost,
wash face, eat cocopops,
Netflix on my laptop,
gotta get a proper job,
bus stop, bus stop, bus stop

bus.

Ripples in the Pond

Jade Marney

I laid with my back on the grass, and my head in the clouds
Daydreaming of the times we were together.
I rolled over; tucked up all cosy in my blankets.
Oh! The warmth that filled my body with joy
But the joy was never lasting.
I lay on my front now, rocking my legs back and forth,
Staring at my reflection in the pond.
And there you were, a perfect Angel in Blue,
Grinning softly back.
"I'm proud of who you've become," you said,
Sending pretty ripples in the water.
And then, in a blink, you were gone

                        And I was left daydreaming again.

Innocence

Tal Rejwan

51.4036224, -0.3026098

Ellen Warner

Violence

Leah Armstrong

Love me violently
The way your mother loved you

With the strength of a thousand suns
Burning the layers of my skin away

To reveal all that's left underneath
To bare my bones to you

The way no one has seen before
Rip me apart to understand me

Make me bleed for you
Writing your name with the blood I've lost

The last words I murmur
A prayer for you.

Peace

Lillian Cowdery

She sat peacefully,
Reaching one hand towards the dry ground,
The other leaning against his obsidian cloak.
His face was a mere pallet of darkness,
Shadows clouding his form,
Yet his soul was pure.
Maybe that is why she idly stroked her hand against the silky fabric of his immortal armour.

Her skin was stark against his powerful black wings,
Yet her auburn hair was unruffled,
As she asked death what it was like to be him.
He gripped his splintered staff,
Beating the ground once. Twice.

Shifting his shadowed hand,
He held her face,
The darkness whispered and caressed her balmy cheek.

He was ice and warmth,
Absence and presence,
Pain and joy,
But not life,
He had never known life.

Only love,
He felt love.
Not from the souls that he had greeted,
But for them.
For her.

He shook his head,
Pain deepening around him,
A tear dropped from his concealed eye.
He did not want her to die.
She smiled at him with such beauty and affection,
Pressing a kiss to his cold lips.
All he could do was grip her fading hand,

And guide her to the other side of the abyss.

"Literature is the most agreeable way of ignoring life."

— *Fernando Pessoa*

SHORT STORIES

The Memory Shop

Rachel Matthews

Eliza Moon had an unusual education.

Whilst other children learned how to add and subtract, Eliza learned how to steal memories. Whilst other children read Austen in English class, Eliza was taught the proper way to label a reminiscence. Whilst other children dissected frogs, Eliza was practising the delicate art of distilling a remembrance into a perfume.

'A memory is a fine, *fine* thing,' her mother would say. 'It is fine in that it is beautiful, and it is fine in that it is fragile. It is a fine, strong thing… until it fades.'

Their house sat at the corner of Hedge End. It was immaculately kept, with white walls, dark oak floors and high ceilings. Attached to the side of the house was a tiny shop. Inside this tiny shop were shelves and shelves of perfume bottles, each labelled with a memory. Her mother's labelling system was precise. The scent of the perfume was listed on the top line, the scene that the memory was associated with on the second and the name of the person to whom the memory belonged on the third.

~ Sea-Salt Breeze and smoke,
BBQ on beach with friends, teenage years,
Marcus Priestly ~

Her mother always hand-wrote the labels herself in spidery, ink-black calligraphy and she always wrapped a deep purple ribbon around the lid.

'Customers expect a certain aesthetic,' she would explain.

Eliza would spend hours watching as her mother organised the bottles so that the right perfumes sat at the front depending on the season. Lavender and chocolate, the scent of first love was a popular purchase on Valentines, whilst fresh snow and gingerbread, the smell of childhood Christmas sold out every time the wind kissed winter.

Any time the bell jingled, Eliza sat up a little straighter as a customer waltzed through the door. She would watch with eager eyes as her mother carefully selected a memory from a shelf and gifted it to a customer. A present, handpicked from the past…

⁓

'Edwina, Edwina darling! I need a perfume that reminds me of youth!' Ms Clements exclaimed.

It was summer and Hedge End was idyllic in it's quiet. The

schools were closed and yet the streets remained empty of youth. The local teenagers preferring to spend time swimming and drinking down by the local river, rather than wandering the same old cobbled lanes. The Memory Shop sat on the edge of things, both a part of the town and yet separate from it.

'How young, Ms Clements?' Eliza's mother asked.

'Oh, young enough to make trouble and enjoy doing so,' Ms Clements sighed. She was a regular to the store and browsed the shelves at leisure. Picking up bottle after bottle with polished red nails. She inspected each label through horn-rimmed glasses. 'I promise I used to live an exciting life; not a day went by without at least one wild adventure. Yet if you were to ask me for a tale from youth, why, I doubt I'd be able to tell you even one exciting thing!'

'A life contains so many moments—it is impossible to remember all of them,' Ms Moon said softly.

With practised fingers, Ms Moon selected a bottle and proffered it to Ms Clements. From behind the counter, Eliza leaned forward, trying to catch a glimpse of which bottle was being sold. Ms Clements blushed, her cheeks flushing to the same colour as her hair.

'Oh, yes! Yes, that's the one!' she cried, rummaging through her purse.

Eliza watched as her mother wrapped the bottle in silver paper and passed it over to Ms Clements in a little purple bag.

The bell above the door jangled once more, Eliza's mother remained facing away from her.

'Eliza, I don't want you spending all your summer behind

this counter. There's a life out there, it's best you go out and live it.'

'But Mum —'

'No buts. One day you will take over this store. What use will you be if you do not know how to create or take a memory? Remember, for a memory to be lost, it first must be *made*.'

Eliza wanted to argue, but she couldn't. Because she knew her mother was right, after all one day she would be the owner of the store. Syphoning off memories and pouring them into glass jars.

At seventeen, Eliza Moon had missed out on a lot of firsts. She had never been on a rollercoaster, yet she knew the sensation well enough - having doused herself one Sunday with the memory of a nine-year-old boy. She had sprayed the perfume against her face and in doing so she had felt the wind in her hair, experienced her stomach do backflips and tasted candyfloss on her tongue.

The Memory Shop had given her more firsts than living a life ever could.

Or so she thought.

'You're the Moon girl, aren't you?'

Eliza nodded, she had been standing by the riverbank for a little over an hour, watching as teens her age jumped in and out of the water. She knew a lot of their names from their visits to the store. Eliza was certain that this girl's name was Sammie Russell and that she'd once bought a bottle containing chilly autumn nights and pumpkin soup.

'Yes,' she replied.

Sammie grinned, and Eliza noticed the gap between her two front teeth. Then she noticed the colour of her hair—red as sunset.

'Well, don't just stand there!' Sammie laughed. 'Come and hang out with us!'

It was that easy.

Without having even tried, Eliza found herself surrounded by people, because of course everyone knew her.

After all, she worked in the Memory Shop.

Sammie was especially delighted by her, asking Eliza question after question about the shop, the bottles, the *memories*. As the summer days passed, these questions shifted slightly, becoming less about the shop and more about Eliza herself.

'What's your favourite kind of memory?' Sammie asked.

They were sitting on the grass beneath one of the many cherry trees that lined the riverbank. Together they watched as Sammie's friends swam in the river—an activity that never grew old in the summer heat. Eliza pulled out a mint leaf from her pocket and popped it into her mouth, shivering with delight as the sweet coolness tingled her tongue. She mindlessly passed one to Sammie, who repeated the action.

'Hmmm,' Eliza said. 'I think memories about people are the best. They're the strongest anyway.'

'How'd you mean?'

Eliza shrugged, 'Well… I guess it depends on the place. A theme park comes with loads of good smells—candyfloss, smoke, hot dogs. But whilst a person might *like* a theme park, they don't *love* it the way they do a home. But the scent of a home is harder to capture, it's almost scent-*less* to the people that live there.'

Sammie nodded along, 'And what about people?'

Eliza pulled the mint leaf from her mouth and pressed it into the dirt. From the river, one of Sammie's friends had jumped into the water, splashing them ever-so-slightly.

Eliza wiped water from her cheek and smiled. 'People always smell of *something*. Cigarettes, sweat, bread. I mean, take this mint leaf, what do you think of when you smell it?'

Sammie chortled. 'You, of course!'

'Exactly! We're wired to associate smells with people. Which is why I always chew mint, it's a nice smell to be associated with.'

Sammie let out a bark of a laugh, 'It's so cool that you know all this!' she said. '*You're* so cool!'

Eliza felt her cheeks grow warm but said nothing.

The summer passed quickly—quicker than any summer Eliza had ever had before. A lazy haze of picnics beneath cherry trees, conversations on riverbeds and marshmallows over open fires.

Sammie made sure that Eliza was involved with *everything*. If there was a BBQ one night, she invited her to it. If the group was going on a bike ride out of town, of course Eliza had to come.

It was glorious.

And every night when she returned home, her mother would ask, 'Have you created a memory today?'

To which Eliza would smile and say, 'Yes.'

And then the question changed. 'Have you *taken* a memory today?'

Eliza fell still, and when no answer was given her mother raised an eyebrow, 'Well, you'd best hurry up. College is about to start soon. Best to nab one quickly.'

Best to nab one quickly.

As if it was as simple as plucking an apple from a tree or grabbing milk from a store.

Still, Eliza nodded and heard the words *'yes, mother'* whispered in a voice that sounded remarkably like her own…

―――

Eliza stood on the riverbank watching from a distance as Sammie's group—although she supposed there were her group too now—kick a ball between them.

Sammie, upon seeing Eliza's silhouette, made her way over.

'Hey, are you not coming down today?'

Eliza shook her head, 'I need to ask a favour…' she stammered. 'I need to ask…'

But she couldn't force the words out, she couldn't bring herself to request such a thing.

A mind is like a labyrinth filled with string, her mother had once said. *You need only find the right thread and pull.*

Eliza placed a shaking hand on Sammie's cheek… and *pulled.*

The riverbank vanished from beneath her feet—the physical world melting away into nothingness. And so Eliza stood inside the maze of Sammie's mind, surrounded by thousands of glorious threads in all types of magical colours—reds, purples, blues, greens. But the thread that shined brightest was a dazzling, fiery orange.

On pure instinct, Eliza grabbed it.

Suddenly a girl's laughter echoed through the labyrinth, whilst a blushing face was projected on every wall.

And everywhere, everywhere, *everywhere* was the heady smell of mint.

Eliza wanted to let go, but she wasn't sure how. She wanted to tug herself free, but she could see no way of doing so without snapping the thread.

And so, in a fumbling, dazed panic—she let it snap.

The labyrinth vanished and Sammie stood blinking before her once more. For a brief, glimmering moment, Eliza thought maybe it hadn't worked after all.

But then she felt the warmth of the memory between her fingers.

'You're that Moon girl, aren't you?' Sammie asked after several seconds had passed.

'Yes,' Eliza mumbled.

Sammie blinked again, her confusion evaporating, 'Do you want to come and hang out with us?'

Eliza balled her hands into fists. The air, previously so still and warm, had a little bite to it now, she supposed summer couldn't last forever.

'Thank you,' she said quietly. 'But not today.'

She turned away, eyes stinging. When she got home, she unfurled her fingers. Inside her right palm glowed a brilliant ball of string—a tiny, orange sun. It burned gently against her skin, the more she stared at it, the more she wanted to hold it close. She leaned forward and inhaled.

There was the sweet smell of cherry blossoms, the cool scent of mint and a touch of damp—it was as though she had never left the riverbed.

It was the scent of her summer and it was ready to be sold.

༺❦༻

Eliza Moon had an unusual occupation.

Out of a tiny shop on the outskirts of Hedge End, Eliza Moon arranged perfume bottles on glass shelves.

Eliza Moon sold memories.

And on a shelf at the back of the store glinted a bottle—a bottle that Eliza hadn't looked at in years.

On the label, in black looped calligraphy, it read:

> ~ *Cherry blossoms and mint leaves,*
> *Young love in summer,*
> *Sammie Russell* ~

It wasn't much; it was only a memory.

But as Eliza Moon often told her customers, a memory is a fine, *fine* thing.

Tall and Quiet and Almost Nothing

Reuben John Loftus

I remember feeling tall. Tall at fifteen. Confronted by two men at five foot nothing, who spoke the words that ended a life I thought I knew.

We were selling the house, a house that woke up to voices pitched at frantic and doors slamming with sound of things needing to be done. We had a viewing and they must have arrived early. My parents running to get everything ready. Silencing creaks and filling holes, straightening picture frames on their nooses and drowning dishes till they squealed perfection; covering the honest mess of a family of five with a layer of contrived normality so people who came to scrub way the history of our life with dreams of their own would think it was worth the investment. But there were no prospective buyers. No nice couple wanting room to stretch out the life that lay ahead of them. Just two men, barely 5 foot nothing who hid under my nose like woodsmen to the oak. Two men who chopped at the ankles of everything I'd ever known and rebuilt the future so backwards and inside out, so different from the one I'd been sure of as to become incomprehensible; a void in the end of forever.

They were plain. They spoke quietly and without hesitation. They were two average men leading ordinary lives who changed the course of everything we knew. Two men who woke up, kissed loved ones goodbye; ate porridge or toast, drove down familiar roads humming tunes in harmony with a thousand commuters to park in usual spots, who clocked in and greeted colleagues, who schemed or gossiped, made tea and coffee in favourite mugs and started a day that to them was much the same as any other. Yet these men at five foot nothing held reality between their hands and with practised motions lifted from pamphlets and seminars, ripped palms apart until our world became nothing; matter became ash, ash to vapour and vapour became the wistful dreams of an adolescent god and each of these men, both barely five foot nothing became free to continue benign days unaware of the destruction they had wrought.

'There has been an accident.'

There was no God or Goliath. No winged messenger or burning bush. No shaking earth or boiling clouds lined with lighting. No triumphant, piteous spectacle to announce the change of all we knew, to announce Ragnarök, Armageddon, the End of times. There was no sign of Al-Masih ad-Dajjal, no Death and his quartet. Only two men in high vis and wet boots murmuring condolences to three new deaf mutes and dog.

'He was dead at the scene, I'm sorry.'

Silence. Less the lack of sound but the abundance of it. Information flooding in so fast and devastating that whatever signals it is supposed to trigger are lost in the commotion, leaving only dead ends and short circuits, wires sparking and writhing seeking connection but finding only void. The aftermath of an explosion that resets experience; a gong struck in concrete box, five foot by five, that rebounds and renounces thought, resonating until it beats into me with its unrelenting rhythm the understanding that it is simply the sound of my mother's heart breaking under the weight of words that should only have been spoken when she had no way to hear them. The silence of a father who must feel he has failed at some test he had been preparing for 22 years. The silence of a sister who will have to be told. The silence of a towering boy, no longer a youth, being confronted by two men, barely five foot nothing who spoke of the ending of life I felt I barely knew.

I see the colours

Melissa Benfalami

You don't own me

Melissa Benfalami

English↔Chinese Romantic Dictionary

(Excerpt\English Version)

Yiran Wei

Something I never told you:

A

Asda is not far from your flat,
I never knew about the supermarket
before I came to your country.

...
C

Cadence of the English sonnet I cannot feel,
how did Shakespeare recite poetry in the wind?

A

'Ai' means love.
How did I write the Chinese word for 'Ai' (愛) ?
The shape of the Chinese character resembles
a net.

...
C

Cai is Napa cabbage. You prefer to eat it.
The Chinese pronunciation of Cai is the same as
the Chinese word for 'money'.

...

E

Elizabeth I II III IV V VI ... are all foreign to me.

Real queens in your motherland. They are not like Disney Queens.

...

E

Er'zi (Son) is better than daughter? Why would someone kill baby girls? Why are top officials all men in a one-party dictatorship in China?

Amy's Ending

Heidi Andreassen

It was a late summer's eve when Amy walked along the river. She looked up at the house she grew up in and felt a tear going down her cheek. *Don't cry,* she thought to herself. She sat down in the cool grass, grasping at the straws, pulling some of the grass up. The grass itched, but she didn't care. She barely even noticed. Her mind was flooded, and beyond that, she noticed nothing. Memories of a troubled childhood flew by her eyes and wallowed in her mind. She could see her mother by the kitchen counter, cooking for the whole family. Her father on the couch, with a half-empty bottle of beer in his hand, and four empty ones on the table. She could see herself hiding in her room with her younger sister, making her be quiet, so there would be no trouble.

If only I hid you better. He would've never found you. The tears kept streaming down her face and her lips had a salty taste because of it. She was only wearing a small, blue tank top and a pair of white shorts, and even though it was summer, her skin was cold to touch. She did not feel herself getting cold, she felt herself getting warm—from anger, hatred, and most of all… loss. She missed her so badly, no words could ever describe it. Ever since she moved away from this place, she had never been to their bedroom—until today. It still looked the same as that day.

Amy laid her head down in the grass, looking up at the sky. There were no clouds, but there were many stars. *Maybe she's up there? Looking down at me?* Amy smiled a little at the thought, but the next minute she thought it was a stupid idea. *Why would she be looking down at me when I couldn't protect her?*

There was a cold breeze against Amy's skin, but she took no notice. She took a deep breath and closed her eyes. Behind her, she heard footsteps. She knew who it was. The man who saved her. The man who would miss her dearly. The one she would leave behind.

'Hey', she said, smiling to him as he laid down in the grass beside her. Her arms were down by her sides, her hands open for grasping. He grabbed her hand and held it tight.

'I'm sorry this has taken such a toll on you', he said. 'I'm never letting you go again.'

She smiled at him and blinked slowly, as she drew her last breath.

A ladybug took off from the rock behind her head and looked down at the pale girl as it flew away. There she was, all alone, lying in the grass. Her eyes staring blankly at the sky. There was no glow left in them, and no colour in her cheeks.

The girl was gone, and a new star was added to the night sky.

The Weight of the Crown

Lucius Strauss

nice to meet you Melissa!!
All the best for your time at Kingston & future!
(Remember, tutors can always be asked for help)

The Influencer

Ross Sullivan

It was an evening in September when my father first announced his intention to hibernate for the winter. He said it casually. The way you might mention that you were thinking of taking up the ukulele. But it landed like a human heart thrown onto the dinner table.

We stared down at our plates, cutlery mid-wield. The only thing that dared move was the dust in the air. But whilst pause enveloped the rest of us, our father continued to tear bread from the loaf at the centre of the table, to corral bechamel and ragù into his mouth, staining the disarranged bristles around it a vivid pomodoro. He told us he would need the extra reserves to sustain him through his torpor as he helped himself to another plateful of our mother's lasagne.

My youngest sister Dorrie started to laugh and then choked on her food. I slapped her on the back and a lump of ground beef flew out of her nose. We all laughed and for a brief moment, we allowed ourselves to believe it was all a joke. But then I looked back towards my father, at the way he fixated on each mouthful. And I started to feel the way you do in a dream where you're climbing a staircase and it becomes impossibly narrow.

We wanted to ask why he'd been gaining weight, why he'd grown his beard so long, why he'd stopped meeting our gaze at the dinner table, why he'd gone from having the frame and nervous energy of our neighbour's old Lurcher, the one that ran out into the road that time, to something more suited to survival in arctic waters. But you don't ask questions that you fear the answer to. Perhaps if our mother's emotional cupboard contained more than carpet cleaner and wood polish she might have talked him out of it rather than just dusting around the problem. Our mother's Land of Oz was reached not by the tornado but by the cyclone generated inside a bagless hoover.

'Yay, Dad's going to hibernate!' Dorrie was only four and to her, this was like your father saying he was going to feature on Octonauts. To her, dad's announcement simply meant that he was now the kill-screen of kindergarten show and tell.

Mum started to clear away the plates, despite none of us having finished our meal. We sat there, our cutlery still in our hands, anaesthetised by the surrealism of it all.

The clatter of crockery loaded aggressively into the dishwasher formed the backdrop to a prickly atmosphere, the charged air before lightning.

'What does that even mean?' Genevieve, who was about to start university, had donned her most treasured look, one of righteous indignation. The one she found more comfortable to wear around the house than a pair of slippers. She looked at each of us in turn, her face a beacon of rage framed by a pixie undercut, imploring us with her polished jade eyes to join her in questioning our father. When she reached me, her gaze seemed to linger.

But it wasn't the same for us. Gen had a lifetime of experience standing up to authority. How did she think we could compete at her level?

When it was clear we weren't capable of the kind of insurrection she was seeking, she left the room without asking permission, muttering words under her breath that we had been brought up not to use. Then our mother returned to extract the cutlery from our hands and bade us to leave the table.

Over the proceeding weeks, divisions coalesced. Dad spent more and more time with Dorrie. He bought her a Dwarf Hamster and told her he was going to make a nest like the ones they made out of straw and cotton wool and the bits of curtains they managed to pull through the bars. He took her on 'foraging' expeditions. They'd be out all day and come home with car-loads of branches and moss they'd collected from God knew where. Dorrie would sit with my father and paint pine cones that she'd collected. I pointed at one, thick with black and brown paint.

'What's that meant to be?' I asked.

'Daddy's faecal plug,' she replied.

He started taking meals in the garage. We only knew he was at home by the muffled rasp of his saw. At night we were kept awake by the banging and the shouting when the hammer missed its target and landed on something soft and full of nerves. When we did see him, it was seldom. On occasion, he came out with blood running down his forearm, his leg or his gut when a new part of his physique had stumbled clumsily into the path of his carpentry; his beard would be beige with sawdust and nut kernels. He was now twice his old weight and his once sinewy limbs the texture and colour of tallow. Once bandaged-up he would retreat back into his cave.

But Mum was grateful for the stains he left in his wake. She absorbed herself in the task of creating poultices from household cleaning products to make our carpets white again.

Genny and I kept our heads down at school, hoping nobody would find out about Dad's ambitions. But the news soon escaped and carried on the air like his weaponised body odour. One evening a man from *the Gazette* called, wanting to write a story. Then the national newspapers caught wind of it. Soon, there were white vans parked along the street adorned with a cityscape of aerials and dishes. Besuited men and women clutching microphones and pieces of paper soon outnumbered residents.

Overnight my father became a cult. He was David Blaine. He was the man who was going to fly over the Grand Canyon in a self-built rocket-powered car. Everyone wanted to see him do it or explode in a ball of flames trying.

Soon influencers picked up the heady chum of unexploited likes. Kids at the back of every class at school were hunkered around videos of Charlie D'Amelio doing the 'Hibernation' dance and memes about my father defecating in the woods. I was permanently caught in a crossfire of furtive glances.

My mother polished the taps in the bathroom for so long that they no longer had any chrome left on them.

Over the following days, frustration and anger gave way to acceptance. Genevieve and I accompanied him on his trips to gather materials. And to our surprise, our father was still the man we remembered him being. We sang songs in the car on the way to the forest. He pointed out weeds that you could eat with peculiar names like 'Jack by the Hedge' and 'Hairy Bittercress'. Although they tasted acrid and vinegary to us, he chewed on them happily as he scoured the underwood for edible mushrooms and wild garlic.

We promised to cook him his favourite foods when we got home. That night we had braised venison with haricots vert and wild morel mushrooms, the following evening honey-glazed pork medallions with goosegrass leaves with garlic mustard, then it was pan-fried bream with celeriac puree and wilted spinach followed by rabbit stew. We ate like Tudors.

Whatever remained on our plate as we sat defeated, we would pass to our father. And he would devour it, morsel by morsel and then lick the plate like one of the snails on the glass of our fish tank.

There was a lake a few miles away where he'd weigh himself down with a bowling ball and stare at me from beneath the water as tench and carp dug around in the silt near his feet. I'd wheel my chair up and down the boards of the jetty watching the seconds tick by on the stopwatch. I sometimes imagined what would happen if he didn't come back up, just disappeared into the darkness, leaving me there on my own by the side of the lake. Alone except maybe for the hundreds of onlookers who followed my dad everywhere he went, like a cloud of drosophila. And then we'd drive home, the car smelling of ammonia from the black mud at the bottom of the pond.

On Halloween morning, he announced that he had stopped eating. *The sudden drop in calories should induce Torpor*, he said and when that happened, he would be ready to go to sleep. *How long would it take?* we asked. He said he didn't know.

My mother started preening him, brushing the knots out of his hair. She insisted that if he was going to do this he should look as decent and respectable as any other animal going into hibernation. It was just as important that he take care of his hygiene if he was going to sit in a hole for weeks on end. Otherwise, goodness knew what he would smell like when he came out. And so, she set about washing him in the bath, the way you would wash a stray dog, shampooing and conditioning his hair and cutting and cleaning under his fingernails. However much she tried to avail him of his beard he insisted it was necessary to retain body heat. She said it made him look old, but she reluctantly allowed him to keep it.

When he came out of the bathroom, he smelled of argan oil and lavender.

Meanwhile, journalists and onlookers from all-over the world maintained their vigil outside, hoping beyond hope that they would get to witness the absurd story's final instalment.

Finally, on Guy Fawkes Night, halfway through a game of Mastermind, he said it was time.

He zipped himself into a hibernation suit. It had been custom-made by a leading skiwear company in collaboration with NASA. A showpiece of breathable waterproof leisurewear, it couldn't quite decide whether it belonged in the clothing aisle or the camping section. As he passed the hall mirror, he regarded himself for a few moments, as if not quite sure who the person looking back at him was. Then he kissed and hugged each of us farewell, in a casual way, the way he used to when he left for work, promising he'd be back in February—March at the latest. *We shouldn't try to disturb him before then.*

We dispersed around the house like identically charged particles. Alone in my room, I thought back to the night of the accident. It was about the same time of year. The roads were slick with icy fur, the night brutally dark; the animal's eyes like balls of lightning, staring us down as Dad spun the steering wheel.

I thought about how difficult it must have been, since that day, as an engineer, to have to spend the rest of his life looking at something he believed he'd broken but was unable to fix.

I still have dreams in which he returns. He just wanders in through the kitchen door, smelling of warm moss and pine needles. But he is slim again, clean-shaven, his hair dark and neatly combed in a side-parting. He is wearing a smart-shirt, like the ones he wore at the factory before it closed. He gives each of us a kiss good morning and then joins us at the table as we all eat together; the way we used to.

Sunk-Cost Fallacy

Julia Jacqueline Clara Tracey

Your cat peed in the sex-box. To be fair, you hadn't cleaned the litter in a day or two.

Counterpoint: you are stressed, manic, your girlfriend is depressed, and the cat should be more understanding.

Regardless, the ethics don't change the fact that somehow, he found the sex-box and also managed to piss in it… The end result is that now, you are on your laptop, in an incognito window, Googling whether or not certain objects can or cannot be appropriately cleansed in order to, in the future, safely interface them with the grungy bits of human anatomy.

You aren't sure whether you are less embarrassed by the fact that countless other people have made the same query, or whether you are going to suffocate under the second-hand embarrassment of the fact that countless human beings needed to Google whether they could purge cat urine from odd bits of assorted rubbers or plastics. You wish you didn't need to know whether they'll infect your junk with some disease that you also never wanted to envision but are currently being forced to speculate on.

Even elbow deep in this situation, you still can't believe your big, chunky cat went and decided to pop a squat on top of the tools whose purpose is to extract a meagre amount of pleasure from the undeniably disgusting human form.

Your current analytical lens is that of cat piss.

What you come to is that it depends on the plastics used, and that some plastics can be scrubbed clean, while others probably shouldn't have penetrated your body in the first place, and you're probably going to get genital cancer at some point in the future. You hope it was worth it and pull up receipts, search through packaging, and find miniature, cat pee encrusted numbers to determine what can be salvaged and what must immediately be disowned. It crosses your mind that if you had acquired sensible degrees and a good job, you could just chuck the whole box and repurchase it, but instead, you are broke, and it was expensive.

There is a sunk-cost fallacy at play. You feel as if you should be able to make a pun on sunk-cost fallacy, but you are embezzled in cat pee. The pursuit of a pun, might in fact, at this point be yet another sunk-cost fallacy.

So instead, you clean. Lathering and rubbing down suggestive surfaces has never been less erotic. Across the house, you can hear the laundry machine clunking away at assorted cloth, rope, or fake-leather goods that were ruined. It's a drumbeat in the background driving the ambiance of the scene. With your hands your suds away the smell, and you sniff the objects of your attention like a bloodhound in search of the tell-tale signs of the crime.

Your cat has decided to watch you do this. Perhaps he is proud of himself. More likely, he just wants you to pet him. Your hands are wet though, and you're still mad, so you don't. You want to believe in your heart of hearts that he knows you are spiteful and angry, but he begins purring, and it's awkward because all you're doing is rubbing down a length of silicone the internet said could be cleansed of danger and scent.

After you're finished, your girlfriend wanders in and asks you what happened, even though you told her earlier.

She'd had headphones in.

You explain the crime scene, and she's disgruntled and says she'll do her own research on whether or not the objects will be safe for human-silicone bonding again.

You know she won't though. That's why you did so much research after all. You had to make sure that the both of you were safe. Research for two.

Still, somehow it turns into a fight and you're tired. The veritable arsenal is now squeaky clean, but you stink of cat pee and the washing machine has now made the house stink of cat pee too. You have to get back to work and the cat is still purring with languid satisfaction.

The scent never comes out of the crap you put in the washer. One or two items are fine—things that were only lightly hit—but the rest goes in a garbage bag. Those items you personally washed like a new-born baby, they are so clean you could eat dinner off them. Probably cleaner.

Your girlfriend never does her own research, but you feel confident.

A Ghost Story

Chloë Bell

I couldn't be on my own in that house anymore, not after what happened. One singular event, sure, but seven different occurrences? No way.

I drum my lilac painted fingernails on my expensive dining table, the one I'd picked up from a vintage market in Greenwich the year before. Back when happiness warmed my heart and my biggest concern was deciphering if the peacock blue armchair, I'd been eyeing up for months, would match my velvet sofa. When I'd been ecstatic, excited beyond belief to own my very first home, a beautiful old cottage surrounded by picturesque countryside. My dream come true.

I continue to tap my fingers. The sound echoes far too loudly, assaulting my ears, making me wince, but I keep doing it anyway.

Everything is too loud at the moment, too much for my mind to comprehend. But then again, that could just be my senses ramping up in intensity, looking for lurking danger. It could also be the fact I was surviving on two hours sleep and copious amounts of caffeine to get through each day. Jittery was my thing now.

'Do you think this will take much longer?' I ask anxiously. There's a hard edge to my voice and it surprises me.

The woman I direct my question at is bustling round my home, picking up objects and studying them. Her beady eyes are scrutinising everything; my possessions, my décor, the feel of the room. She lifts her head and sniffs like she's assessing the stifling air. Suddenly it's far too cold in the room and I shiver, pulling my knitted cardigan around me, crossing my arms.

I gulp down my worry and watch her, eager for an answer, but the woman just shrugs, her back to me.

I pick at a loose thread on the sleeve of my cardigan and gaze at her, trying to guess what kind of person she is. Is she a *fraud*? Am I paying her for nothing? Is this idea, my last resort, utterly insane?

The woman I make assumptions about is wrapped in a long black dress that skims the cold stone floor when she walks. Bangles jingle irritatingly on her arms when she moves, her presence is unsettling, and I can't put my finger on why.

She is probably in her late fifties or early sixties, but I've never been great at guessing ages. She has long, dark hair with beads weaved through random sections and when the lights above catch her strands, silvery threads of grey sparkle.

She takes a notebook out of the canvas tote bag she has looped over her shoulder and finally glances at me. I cannot read her expression, but she speaks in a deadpan tone.

'Do you have a pen?'

I note her voice is croaky; she must be a smoker; I decide in my head. Without a word, I sweep over to my desk in the corner of the room and scoop up a discarded biro. Handing it over, I try to judge if she thinks the situation is *bad* or not. Has she seen this kind of thing before? Am I a whole new case?

Panic rises in my throat and I gulp it back down. My hands begin to shake.

I can't live here anymore, I just can't. I'm not safe. I don't really want this woman here, rifling through my things, but I also suddenly don't want her to leave either. I don't want to be alone in here. My vision starts to blur and I blink, trying to clear my mind and my eyes as they well up with frustrated tears. Am I just imagining it all, like Sophie said? No, I can't be, *can I?*

'Coffee?' I ask, my voice coming out as a high-pitched squeak. I need to do something with my hands, occupy my brain to stop it unravelling like the sleeve of my jumper.

'Camomile tea, please. If you have it.'

I nod and bustle into the kitchen without a word, grabbing two mugs from the overhead cupboards. Flicking on the kettle, I steady myself, both hands on the countertop. I breathe in and out slowly. In through my nose, out through my mouth, I unhunch my shoulders and feel myself physically relax. That's when I hear the scream from the next room. It bounces off the hard, unforgiving walls and my blood runs cold, like ice.

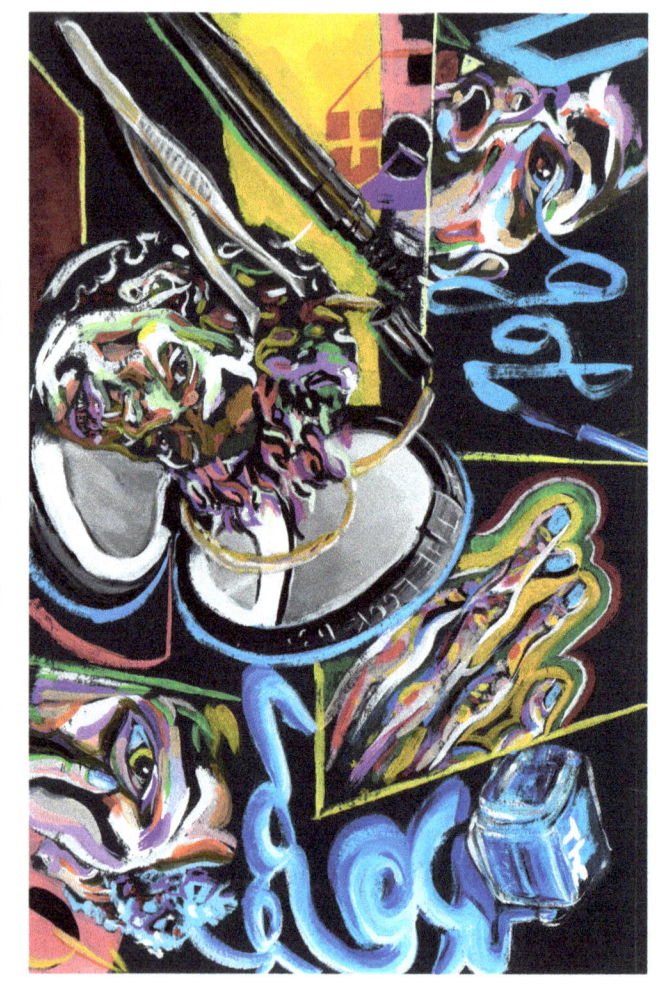

U got the Look

Luca Serra

Watercolour & Braid Fits

Luca Serra

The Dead Were Never from Florida

Xyvah M. Okoye

The dead were never from Florida. But I supposed it could not be helped.

Sighing, I propped my elbows upon the low, red-draped mahogany table before me and slouched forward to rest my chin on my interlaced knuckles. To my left and right, twin flames flickered on the thick red candles burning in bronze bowls on the table—the only light within the red taut canvas of my domain. 'And when did she leave this plane?' I asked the black dressed man before me.

He took pains to flatten the lapels of his peacoat with his leather-gloved hands and cleared his throat, but the tremor in his voice was unmistakable as he said, 'Exactly three months now, ma'am.' He squirmed on the velvet cushions, clearly unused to sitting cross-legged on the floor. I fought the smile tugging my lips upwards. He was unlikely to notice my expression with the gossamer silk shawl draped over my head and covering all but my eyes, but I was a professional and that demanded some level of… discipline.

Keeping my voice neutral, I asked, 'Did you bring an item of hers?'

The man nodded a little too fervently. Shoving a hand into his coat, he teetered as he retrieved a small item wrapped in a white silk handkerchief. He held it over the table, hand trembling, fingers remaining curled around the object. 'I was told the dearer it was to her, the stronger the connection would be.' He inhaled deeply and let the air out through his mouth before finally placing the item on the table between us. 'I hope this is enough.'

A faint buzzing filled the tent.

The man cast weary glances about him before his gaze finally returned to settle on me. 'Will it work?'

I scrunched my face up into a most convincing look of consideration before nodding curtly and sitting up straight. With a gesture of practised grace, I swiped up the offering, feeling the solid round shape of it as I stashed it within the heavy folds of my red robes. There was no point checking the item. Judging by the man before me; by his slicked back coppery hair and slanted green eyes, by his finely tailored clothes and the way he clenched and unclenched his fists in his lap, like he needed to be in control. The goods were definitely authentic. And very, very valuable.

'Let us begin.' I cleared my throat and raised both hands high above my head.

The man watched, caution dancing in his emerald eyes. This time, I indulged in a smile. He had travelled all the way from Austin for this. The least I could do was give him a good show.

The chant began softly. Like a whisper on the wind, it whistled from me, growing as it filled the red tent. The candlelight danced lazily to the tune; a tune it had grown used to—I had grown used to—over the past half-decade. Before me the man stared, his face creasing with what looked like suspicion.

Perhaps a little more theatrics then.

I raised my voice, the chant barrelling out of me with the determination of a typhoon. The flames leaped, the wax beneath them hissing. Swirling tendrils of smoke rose from them to snake about the room. The man flinched, but otherwise kept his composure.

'Is any of this really necessary?' he asked.

'Do you wish to commune with your dead wife?' I shot back.

He recoiled, his thin lips pursing into a tight line.

Good.

I closed my eyes and waved my hands, wiggling my fingers as I lowered the timbre of my voice in a bid to sound ominous. The faint buzzing grew steadily until it hummed along to my chant like a flat, out of tune note struck on a piano forte.

This time, the man jounced in his seat. At the sounds of his shuffling and the hissing fabric of the cushion, I cracked open an eyelid. He turned at the waist, searching the shadowy corners of the tent for what only he knew.

'She's here,' I whispered, seizing the chance. At the suddenness of the change he spun to face me, his pale face contorted in terror.

'Where?' he blurted. 'Where is she?'

Lowering a hand, I pointed to the far-right corner which was cast completely in shadows. His gaze followed my finger point. 'There,' I said slowly, ominously. 'She's right there.'

'Ebony?' The man scrambled away from the corner so terrified that he did not register when he knocked the table back. I barely had time to grab the swaying, tittering candles and jump out of the way before the whole thing toppled over.

Staring down at the table at my feet, I cursed under my breath. There's always that customer who makes a mess of things, I suppose.

But the ruse had to go on.

After taking a steadying breath, I whispered, 'Your late wife wishes to know why you summoned her from her rest.'

'Ebony,' the man sobbed. 'You're here, my love.' His shoulders heaved with the weight of his grief as he bowed his head, buried his face in his palms and wept.

A part of me felt a little sorry for him. Another depraved part, twisted by greed and suffering, considered extorting him some more. Choosing to ignore both parts, I watched on, awaiting my cue.

Time crawled painfully by, moment by sobbing, sputtering moment as I waited, wondering what sort of love would drive such a man to such lengths. Seeking out the means to commune with his dead wife was one thing, actually employing such means was another. But weeping and slobbering like a simpering oaf? Now that was entirely different.

Three parts bored and seven parts curious, I said, 'Ebony wishes to know why you have summoned her.'

It worked. The sound of my voice seemed to pull the man back to the present. He straightened his back and dried his cheeks with the heels of his palms. 'I came—" He cleared his throat. 'I came to apologise.'

My brows rose with interest. 'Go on.'

He turned and shot me a dirty look before quickly turning back to face the dark, empty corner of the tent.

I grinned beneath my shawl. What a fool.

'I know we did not always see eye to eye,' he continued, his voice gaining strength with each word. 'We disagreed on most things, to be quite frank. I was the superior chess player. You were so lousy at it that even letting you win was such a difficult task to accomplish. You could hardly tell which pieces were which, let alone how they moved.' He cleared his throat and flattened his lapels. 'Still, you never listened when I set you right. What else was I supposed to do if not teach you a lesson?'

A slight discomfort crept over me, but I stilled myself and schooled my features into the placid calm that was expected of me. It wasn't uncommon to encounter an odd client or two. Besides, I had seen... odder. I could remain non-judgemental.

'Well,' he said and cleared his throat once more. 'Well, I hope you learned your lesson.' He sighed. It was a heavy, sorrowful sound. 'I only—' his voice cracked with emotion, and he took a well-needed moment to calm himself before continuing. 'I just wanted you to admit that you were wrong, and I was right. Just… Just once, Ebony. You were a terrible chess player and I knew you would never admit it, just as you would never admit you were a lousy cook.' He chuckled. 'I suppose if you were any good in the kitchen then you'd still be here…'

A contemplative silence followed his words, then he cleared his throat once more, rolled his shoulders back, straightened his jacket and quipped, 'Well, the sodium fluoroacetate is gone, the salt is back in the cupboard and I wanted to let you know I'm sorry. I am terribly sorry about your current predicament and, if it is any consolation, your epitaph reads:' he raised a hand, pinching his thumb and index fingers together as he waved like a conductor '—Always remember: the opponent whose king has been checkmated has lost the game.'

Where It Cuts Deep

Rachel Matthews

When I was young I believed in stories about hope. I clung to them the way a little girl might cling to her mother's skirts. I believed that monsters could always, always be defeated and that everyone would live happily ever after.

As I grew up, the narrative began to change. The way I viewed the world twisted this way and that, until the shape was different. Eventually, the hope was… not exactly gone, but it didn't shine quite as bright.

This is not the story I wanted to tell, but it is *my story*.

This is me, carving my heart out with a pen and giving it to you, dear reader. Words, ink and memories. I have nothing else to give.

'So, before we start I just need to confirm your —'
'Kayleigh Forrest, 2nd September 1995.'

The nurse smiled kindly. 'I take it you've done all this before?'

Obviously. 'Yeah, a few times.'

That was underselling it. Three years of living with Crohn's disease and it felt like I spent more time in hospitals than outside of them. Despite being told that the disease was incurable I had been hopeful at first—confident even—that I would get better.

I didn't.

I was so thin back then. My face so gaunt that I more closely resembled a skeleton than a girl, my wrists so brittle they looked as though they might snap with one good hard shake. I simply couldn't hold food down. I tried—God knows I tried—yet still I was wasting away in front of the mirror every damn day. There was nothing I could do to stop it. I pictured myself as a shiny, red apple slowly being eaten away on the inside by a fat, disgusting worm.

I'd been on steroids, I'd been on drugs to lower my immune system, I'd been on crazy-horrible liquid diets where I wasn't allowed to eat anything for three months…and nothing worked. The doctors started to throw around words like 'aggressive' and 'drug resistant.' It became all too clear that all the treatments had simply been delaying the inevitable.

This.

We sat in a small box room; the nurse, my boyfriend, my mother, and myself. But I was the only one draped in a hospital gown, complete with ridiculous knee-high socks. Simon sat beside me, his hand resting on my knee and his foot tapping persistently on the floor. He watched carefully as the nurse wrapped the blood pressure monitor around my arm. There was also my mother, draped in black with her hair ironed out smooth. She was all fire, a match ready to burn.

'Will we get to see the surgeon before she goes in?' Mother demanded.

The monitor squeezed around my arm, a gentle numbing throb.

'No, I'm afraid not. But the anaesthetist will be in shortly and she should be able to answer all your questions,' the nurse had a kind face and warm voice. But I knew it would be an insufficient shield and would not protect her from my mother's wrath.

'I really don't think that's good enough. Mr North should see us beforehand so that he can answer all our questions!'

'Mum,' I said softly. 'We know all the answers already.'

My mother's nostrils flared, and her lips turned into a thin, thin line. She didn't say anything else, but she didn't need to, her silence said it for her. Simon's grip tightened on my knee.

'It'll be alright,' he said. 'We're prepared, ain't we?'

I nodded. 'Damn straight.' I smiled, but the smile felt stretched out and false across my face. My heart was pounding so hard as though it was trying to break free of my ribs. Simon was right, we had been preparing for months—years even. My eyes flitted to the clock.

Twenty minutes to go.

The nurse wrote down my blood pressure, 'It's a little low.'

I shrugged; it always was. Then she took my temperature

and exited the room quietly.

'How ya feelin'?' Simon asked as soon as the door was shut.

'Nervous.'

'You'll be fine,' Mum said sternly. 'You're a warrior. Just like your damn mother.'

I nodded again—it seemed the only thing to do.

'What are you going to do whilst I'm under?' I asked.

'We're just going to grab some lunch at that little pub around the corner,' Mum said. 'They'll call us as soon as you're done.'

'I should be in the green zone, either the Nightingale or Northumberland Ward,' I recited.

Simon smiled; I could have lived in the crooked edges of that smile. 'We know babe, we'll be there when you wake up.'

The anaesthetist entered the room, she sat down and was immediately bombarded with questions from my mother. I can't remember the questions or the answers. Only the clock counting down the seconds and Simon's foot tap, tap, tapping on the floor.

'Are you ready?'

I stood up, 'Yep.' In that instant, my voice didn't sound like my own, or rather I didn't remember speaking the words, only hearing them. We were led out into the corridor and to a set of large blue doors.

'This is where she has to leave you, I'm afraid,' the anaesthetist said. I hadn't noticed before, but she was an attractive woman and French from the soft lilt of her vowels. I realised with a jolt that I didn't even know her name. I was placing my life in her hands and I *did not know her name*.

Mum grabbed me by the shoulders and pulled me into a crushing hug.

When I turned to say goodbye to Simon, I could see he was red in the face; his eyes were watery but not quite crying.

'See you on the other side,' I grinned again.

I hoped they couldn't see me shaking.

I remember walking down a wide corridor and past rows of silver lockers. I remember the strong, acidic smell of chemicals. I remember the room; white, small and unnervingly empty. I could feel my breathing getting heavier and heavier as I sat on the table. The anaesthetist withdrew the epidural, the longest needle I had ever seen and it was plunged like a sword into the base of my spine. My legs stopped shaking—I couldn't move.

I remember being laid down.

'Okay now, sharp scratch.'

A tiny prick on the back of my hand.

The light hanging from the ceiling glowed brighter, brighter, *brighter*.

And then everything burned yellow.

I'd like to say that the surgery fixed everything but as I said earlier, this isn't the story I would *like* to tell.

I was placed under the knife and I temporarily rose victorious, the disease cut out of me. Half a colon had been snipped away and in its place, there was a stoma; a pink tongue poking out on the left side of my stomach. The pain—the never-stopping, ceaseless, crippling *pain*—had been erased.

I could leave the house. I could eat! And I revelled in every delicious moment of it.

A year later the walls came crashing down all over again.

My surgery, life-saving and wonderful as it was, had resulted in the swelling and destruction of my fallopian tubes. One more piece of me had been broken, one more piece needed to be sliced away and with it, the ability to ever conceive children naturally.

When I was told the news, I experienced a surreal, dreamlike moment. My mind traced itself back to the moment that this particular story began, the story of Kayleigh Forrest, a woman with Crohn's disease.

I felt like, maybe, that's all I was now. Like all the other versions of myself that *could have been*, were gone. Snuffed out like candles one by one, leaving behind only smoke.

The monster, that ugly worm inside of me, had somehow trapped me again.

Monsters. We all have an idea of what that word should mean, the old witch in the gingerbread house, the fallen angel with devil's wings. We've heard the tales and we know the warning signs, but the truth is that the worst monsters are the ones we can't see, the ones that can't be defeated by the swing of a sword or by true love's kiss.

The monster in my story is never going away.

This is not the life I planned on living, but here I am, living it anyway.

So, what do you do when the scars that hurt the most are the ones that run deeper than the skin? What do you do when the life you dreamed of is wiped away as easily as chalk from a blackboard?

How do you *live*?

I'll tell you.

You twist the shape of your life and you mould it into something new. You dream new dreams. You find new hope. You create *new* stories.

Why? Because that's all there is.

Legs in Butter

Deborah Thompson

Once upon a time, a princess was wandering in the garden, thinking of supper, when she met a frog, croaking peacefully in the wet grass beside the pond.

Her first thought was, 'Oh goody, I must tell Cook,' (the Princess was very fond of frog's legs), and then she noticed, with a stab of disappointment, the little golden crown perched on the frog's green head.

The frog, his vision clouded by dreams of cool mud and juicy flies, finally noticed the Princess, and his little green heart sank.

Oh look, I've met a princess, he thought frogly. *It was bound to happen one day, wasn't it? After all, it's what I've been waiting for all these years. Isn't it?*

The Princess was thinking exactly the same thing. After all, everyone knows that a princess isn't a real princess without a frog prince to kiss, rescue and marry. Is she?

'Well,' she said to the frog, wondering why she was feeling

so reluctant. 'There's no use in wasting any time. I suppose we'd better get on with it?'

'*Yes, I suppose so,*' said the frog Prince, valiantly trying to banish thoughts of cool water and lush green lily pads, and raised his shiny head obediently. After the slightest of hesitations, so slight that only her mother would have noticed, the Princess planted a quick kiss on his forehead, and lo! Before her stood a handsome prince.

Well, a prince, anyway. There was something still quite, well, *froggy* about him, she couldn't help feeling, even in human form.

His mouth stretched from side to side.

His eyes were very widely spaced.

His nose was very flat.

As she watched, his mouth opened, and a long thin tongue flicked out and expertly caught a passing fly.

The Prince blushed guiltily and swallowed the fly with a hasty gulp. He didn't quite know what to do next, so he twiddled his long thumbs and shuffled his feet uncomfortably in the mud. It was then that the Princess noticed his legs. Clothed though they were in gilded finery, there was no disguising the fact that they were long, green and thin, and his feet, though shapely, were webbed.

No one, not even her mother, could deny that they were a frog's legs.

The Princess thought about her mother and the delight she would feel when she heard about this encounter.

'Darling!' Mother would say. 'Well done! High time! I'm

so proud of you! So what if the Prince hops! So what if any passing fly is doomed! Nobody's perfect, and the sooner you realise that the better. Besides, you can always train him out of his bad habits when you're married. The important thing is that now you can fulfil your destiny!'

The Princess thought about her destiny. And about duty. And about expectations. She even thought about love.

She noticed how the Prince's eyes kept sliding longingly over to the pond, even as he was kissing her hand.

She thought about his long green legs.

She wondered if he would ever really change.

'Prince,' she said. 'I don't think this is a great idea, do you?'

The Prince blushed again, this time bright green with relief.

'Are you sure?' he asked. 'I mean, I'd be happy to marry you, of course…'

'No, really, that's all right,' said the Princess .

'Well,' said the Prince, who was shrinking with a speed he hoped wasn't too rude. *Only if you're sure…*

He hopped way toward the damp heaven that was his home.

The Princess turned to face her mother's wrath. She knew she'd made the right decision.

She definitely didn't want to spend the rest of her life fighting the temptation to sauté his legs in butter.

Crow, Devil, God

Phoebe Levins

There is a dead crow on the long stretch of road between her house and school.

She still doesn't know how the crow died, even after an entire week since the first time she noticed it. It wasn't a busy road at all, so it couldn't have been a car accident. In fact, home was three miles away from the town, so at least two miles away from anyone else. People didn't come towards Ruth and her grandmother's place to shoot, so it couldn't have been that either. Apparently, their soil was cursed or their farm was haunted, or some other uneasy imagined evil to make them stay away.

Ruth stared down at it. The first time she'd seen the dead crow, it had been almost pristine. She'd seen a lot of crows. Crows on their fields were her grandmother's worst nightmare. She'd even seen a few dead ones. So it wasn't particularly a surprise to find one on the side of the road on that hot August day. They'd said it was the hottest August in the last ten years.

Ruth believed it.

The crow seemed unaffected. Just dead. Ruth had adjusted to the idea of death at a very young age anyway. All the children in town did. They all went to church and prayed for something different—obviously something shiny and golden and saving. Ruth wasn't all too sure about that. She was sure of death, though. So the dead crow hadn't really provoked much interest in her.

She walked past the crow for an entire week before she decided to investigate its black body properly.

It was no longer pristine after a week. It seemed to have been half torn apart in some blip of time between Ruth's walk from school yesterday and her walk to school that morning, like it had died in a much worse way than she'd originally thought.

Its guts had crawled out of its tiny stomach and rested, exposed, on the short dead grass. Tiny entrails and ruby blood, almost alive with savage little insects. She'd missed observation of the carrion flies moving in, although that was rarely observed casually, as they descend upon and begin to devour and populate a carcass minutes after it hits the ground for the last time. They had already made their home in the soft feathers of the crow, laid their eggs, and eaten the tiniest inches of flesh. The larvae had already begun to gather at the skull, wriggling in the dry dirt and sharing a feast of epic brain matter like a Thanksgiving dinner. They'd already torn through its dark eyeball, and she could see them pushing out around its sclerotic ring. Ruth was almost disappointed that she'd missed the chance to see the beginning of the colony.

She supposed that yes, the crow was just dead, but here it was, housing an entire extended family of little bugs.

It wasn't just the flies, though. Ruth might have missed the flies, but she crouched down soon enough to see the beginnings of the second step. The carrion beetles had also encroached. They were the most impressive. They had started tearing bigger parts of the crow off, but the beetles would also eat the flies and their larvae in an attempt to eradicate their competition. Ruth leaned closer, tucking her skirt between her legs and shaking her hair out of her face for a closer look. The smell could reach her then. It turned her stomach. Strong, acidic, and disgusting. Forcing its way up her nose and down her throat, making her cough against the strength of it.

She watched them carefully tearing apart the bird, like synchronised swimmers who had been practising for years. This was their big show, and they were doing an amazing job. The crow was being emptied out—gutted like a childhood home. They were together and they were competing, just like she'd been taught and witnessed herself too many times for 14 years. Their job would be done quickly and cleanly and soon enough she wouldn't even be able to tell which part of the road the crow had been lying.

The decomposers moved fast, almost desperately and it looked like the whole crow was vibrating. Ruth found herself leaning even closer, her hands hitting the dusty ground in front, inches away from the corpse. It really did look like it was moving. It's chest especially. She could see it moving- heaving as if the lungs inside still worked. As if it wasn't dead at all. Up and down and up and down and slowly, steadily, like a half-asleep man. The yellow worms crawled frantically around its exposed intestines and the crow breathed.

Ruth's chest tightened, eyes wide, but unable to look away. Unable to move at all. She could only watch as it breathed. She inched closer and closer and decided not to worry about the way grandmother would complain about her dirty knees and dusty skirt and how she'd probably be in for a good few slaps when she got home. She only cared about the breathing, dead crow. She stared at its face, encased in maggots and missing most of it's eye. It's sclerotic ring had been polished to smoothness.

She leaned so close she could almost hear it, so close her eyes started to water from the smell of digestible flesh, so close that the bugs went out of focus and it was just her, the breathing crow and its blood-matted black feathers. Her and the crow and the wind. It carried on breathing.

'Ruth.'

At the same time a carrion fly landed on the back of her hand and she screamed louder than she had before. She hoped it was the wind. It sounded much more sinister than the wind. She ran until her throat burned and her tears had stopped.

Pray for something shiny and gold and saving. She overturned prayers in her head as she ran, too out of breath to speak them aloud.

O Lord, I commit my life to your hands. Send your angels to guide and protect me in the day and the night, in the name of Jesus.

O Lord, my life is in your hands; please cover me with your feathers.

O Lord, O Lord, O Lord.

But she could still hear it over her desperation. Like it was following her. Her stomach turned. It only got louder.

'Ruth. Ruth. Ruth.'

Shiny and gold and saving.

Think, saviour. Think, safety. Think, God will save You. Think, believe in him.

Ruth threw up on the street when she reached the town. She vomited until it was only soft white foam and then a little more for good measure. The voice had stopped echoing now; her head was finally and thankfully, absolutely silent. But her throat burned and every hair on her body stood frozen upright.

The memory of the voice was strong and played softly in the background in her mind the whole day, driving her mad. It was difficult to convince herself it'd been fake when she could still hear it. It was dark and deep, chilling to the core. She wasn't sure it was the crow. It was in her head, disembodied, like the Wizard of Oz. It rang loud in her skull and made her nauseous. The depth of it making her feel as though she was falling backwards into inexplicable darkness every time she closed her eyes and imagined it. It played like a broken record all day.

No one said anything because no one ever said anything to Ruth. Her frightened and pale look was hardly out of the ordinary to anyone else. She sat by herself at lunch like usual, although she couldn't stomach the cornbread she'd taken for lunch and tried to drown out the repeated call of her name with Bram Stoker's Dracula.

It barely worked.

The real issue would be walking home. There was no other way to her house but up the long, dusty road.

I bled with bleach, cleansed and eroded my soul, with two horns I now stand more alive than ever, that death was needed to guide my breath to the beat of my Creator's command.

Two Horns

Saleha Bakhtiar

Grief

Ruairidh MacLean

Grief was a young man who once ate an apple, not just the flesh, but the core, the stem and the seeds. After a short amount of time he began to feel a pain in his stomach and he realised that an apple tree had taken root inside him. Grief went to see a doctor, but the doctor was only able to confirm the quickening of the apple tree and could offer no solution to the problem. The doctor said simply:

'The tree will grow until it is too great to be contained by your body, Mr. Grief and at that time your life will come to an end.'

At first Grief was utterly distraught, he could do nothing but cry and rage for days on end. Many friends and family members would approach him and try to calm or console Grief—but he was beyond consoling. After about a week, the pain in his stomach had become quite acute, and he could feel a tight, solid knot inside himself. When he spoke or exhaled heavily, his breath smelled of freshly cut grass and dry leaf mould. He became furious with the thing growing inside him and rose from his state of howling collapse to one of manic action.

He attempted to kill the tree by imbibing almost boiling water, which surprisingly he was able to survive largely unscathed—unfortunately so was the intestinal plant. When this failed, he consumed weed killer at a dose that made him deathly ill, but was short of killing him. He shat out blood with his faeces, green verdant leaves and slivers of bark. But the knotted bands continued to grow and spread inside him.

At last Grief attempted to cut the thing from himself with a knife. With some effort and a surgical blade, Grief found he could cut open his own belly and reach inside—but the roots of the stomach-tree had wrapped themselves tightly about Grief's internal organs. Every tug on the belly roots led to a sharp sensation as the branches pulled at his heart. At last Grief admitted defeat, and after stitching himself up, he lay down on his bed and did not move or speak for some time.

He did not find the spreading tendrils of the tree painful anymore—but regarded them with dispassionate curiosity. He first noticed how the branches began to coil around his limbs, stiffening them and causing them to bulge in textured rings. He felt the leafy canopy begin to creep up through his oesophagus where it tickled the back of his throat. After about a week, parts of the tree had begun to grow out of his orifices—his urethra and anus bristled with long, fibrous sub-roots and even if he had wanted to speak he could not, for his mouth was completely stuffed with crooked little branches festooned with delicate leaves.

He began to find his ears were filling with a pulsing thump—which he realised was the rhythm of the tree's systolic system. The canopy had at last stretched up and colonised his skull.

A couple of days later, a beautiful white bud blossomed on one of his mouth branches. Spring had begun outside and Grief realised he didn't have long left. With the last, fading portion of his strength he fought against the inflexibility of his timberous limbs and shuffled out of his bed. With a heroic effort, he managed to struggle into his garden, out to the soiled banks at its head. Here he let his feet sink into the ground, the double weight of man and tree driving him into the earth. Slowly, the sun set. By morning there would be no more Grief, only an apple tree in a garden.

This Year's Creatives

Joshua Ciccone
Joshua Ciccone is currently studying English Literature at Kingston University. He is interested in the Fantasy and Science-Fiction genres, as well as Victorian Literature. He finds inspiration from mythology and other fairy-tales.

Kathleen Fairweather
Kathleen Fairweather was born in Lausanne, Switzerland, to South African parents and grew up there until she moved to London five years ago. She loves spending time in the woods, mountains, and lakes. Kathleen especially enjoys reading and - having been inspired by Emily Dickinson - her first ambition was to be an author.

Zeynep Zee Sertkaya
Zeynep Zee Sertkaya is a second-year Psychology student. She is a bullet journalist, bookworm and nature lover. This piece is from her lockdown days when she used art to keep herself sane throughout the pandemic.

Rakhi Kohli
Rakhi Kohli has always had a passion for sports, having taken part in competitive martial arts for six years and boxing for a

further two. She is also a national level swimmer! Rakhi has an unhealthy obsession with Lilo and Stitch, the colour blue and her three adorable dogs. She hopes to one day own a huge farm to rescue unloved animals.

Lillian Cowdery
Lillian Cowdery is a second-year student at Kingston University, studying Journalism and Media BA Hons. She is passionate about writing poetry and short fictional stories, and had a poem published in an under sixteen competition when she was twelve. She also has news writing, poetry, and other creative writing experience.

Jad H. Al Shara'a
Jad H. Al Shara'a is an overly ambitious, young Syrian international law student interested in literature and seeking resolve in making his thoughts and emotions heard through words.

Shreyash Pant
Shreyash Pant is from India. Despite being from a technical background, Shreyash was always connected to creativity. He loves to take impromptu photos while exploring new places.

Greta Jonas
Originally from Minnesota, Greta Jonas moved to London without ever having been before. She graduated from the University of Roehampton in 2022 with a first-class degree in

Creative Writing and is now pursuing an MA from Kingston University in Creative Writing and Publishing. Greta currently works at a small indie press as a freelance editor. In her free time, she enjoys drinking oat cappuccinos, watching trashy reality TV and petting street cats.

Mekhla Paul
Mekhla Paul is a writer by profession and an artist by passion. Shen is an enthusiastic person who finds joy in small things and takes inspiration from real life incidents. She is a fantasy lover who writes stories and scripts to delve deeper into the depths of creative writing while creating a sense of happiness for herself and her readers. She self-published her first novel called 'The Alpha's Alyne' and a few poems in numerous anthologies.

Saida Adila binti Sukman
Saida Adila binti Sukman is an MA Publishing student who loves to write original stories, fanfictions and book reviews.

Ezgi Gürhan
Having previously worked as the Editor-in-Chief for the publication of Creel 5: An Anthology of Creative Writing, Ezgi Gürhan decided to study an MA in Creative Writing and Publishing at Kingston University. As a writer, poet and avid reader, she is interested in mythology, fairy tale retellings and all things fantasy.

Margaret Schnekenburger

Margaret Schnekenburger is an exchange student from Canada. She majors in Psychology and minors in Gender Studies. She mainly kept her writings to herself, given they are often personal and a form of releasing unwanted feelings. She adores poetry and short essays and took a chance at RiPPLE. Her writings represent the struggle of femininity and feminine anger.

Patricia Mercado

Patricia Mercado is a part-time Creative Writing and Publishing Master's student. Her love for poetry started with the great Sylvia Plath and lately, she finds herself heavily inspired by Ocean Vuong. She hopes to one day be able to share her work with literally anyone, other than her pretend audience at home.

Felix Orlo

Felix Orlo is a queer performance poet, comedian and Creative Writing MA student based in Camden, London. She's the Creative Director of The Bobolyne Poets, a punk poetry collective that performs at festivals such as Brighton Fringe, Camden Fringe and FUSE International. Felix is also co-parent to Sheena's House of Fun, an alternative stand-up night that raises money for refugee charities. Her spoken word is often combined with music and moving images in a mischievous, tongue-in-cheek voice. She is published with Hysteria Zine, Spun Press and Tooothgrinder Press.

Jade Marney
Jade Marney is currently studying Creative Writing MA on a part-time basis. Their favourite pastimes are to read, write and listen to music. Previously, they have had a poem published in the school anthology and received first prize for the poem. In the future, they are working towards publishing their first novel.

Tal Rejwan
Writer, artist, reader and dreamer, Tal Rejwan has previously illustrated the cover for Creel 5 and the Hebrew editions of the Tear Asunder series by Nashoda Rose. After working at Graff Publishing as a social media manager, she decided to pursue her long-life dream of becoming an author and taking on a bigger role in the publishing industry. She completed a Creative Writing BA at The University of Essex and is currently studying a Creative Writing and Publishing MA at Kingston University.

Ellen Warner
Ellen Warner's work is inspired by Zarina Bhimji's photographs and the element of "location of light"; their practice examines the quiet details of our surroundings that go unnoticed each day. Photography is their means of research; embarking on a journey and shooting film helps them to engage with their surroundings. To observe and record fleeting moments of light and shadow.

Leah Armstrong

Leah Armstrong is a third year Creative Writing student at Kingston University. Poetry is one of her favourite muses to let out all feelings. Someday, she hopes to write stories all over the world.

Rachel Matthews

Rachel Matthews is a bookworm with an unhealthy addiction to coffee and chocolate eclairs. She lives with her husband and dog in the not-so-sunny seaside town of Worthing. Rachel's biggest dream in life is to have a novel published – her second biggest dream is to one day own a very expensive coffeemaker.

Reuben John Loftus

Reuben Loftus is a diarist writer from Cumbria with a diverse background travelling the world and working as a chef, musician, ski-instructor, cattle farmer, door-to-door salesman and barman. Currently working on completing his MA in Publishing, Reuben is a freelance editor and writer trying to put some of his words to paper.

Melissa Benfalami

Melissa Benfalami is a first-year architecture student from Algeria. She is a 19-year-old artist who is open to experimenting with different mediums and tools. The drawings published are made with oil pastel. This is also her first artwork to be published.

Yiran Wei

Yiran wants to leave you speechless with her passionate words while sharing her experience from living in a totalitarian state. She wishes to create a sense of confusion and greed with her writing style.

Heidi Andreassen

Heidi is a 25-year-old student from Norway, currently pursuing a master's degree in Creative Writing. The best year of her life (so far) was spent on a one-year study programme in Creative Writing, with two published authors as teachers. Writing has always been a passion she wanted to pursue.

Lucius Strauss

Lucius Strauss is a queer Level 6 Illustration Animation student from Germany. He enjoys a wide variety of creative practices but prefers to always insert an aspect of surrealism and whimsy into his works. Lucius is currently studying Korean and presenting LGBTQ+ workshops alongside his course. He is passionate about language and cultural exchange, as well as food.

Ross Sullivan

Ross Sullivan is a full-time MA student studying Creative Writing. He hopes to become a novelist. He studied Biology as an undergraduate, so his writing tends to involve playing with scientific concepts.

Julia Jaccqueline Clara Tracey

Julia is a queer writer focusing on the LGBTQ+ fiction genre at its foundations. She mostly writes prose fiction because of this, but over time she has developed a deep and abiding love of nonfiction essays, particularly flash nonfiction. A couple of her poems were published in Headwaters magazine in 2019.

Chloë Bell

Chloë Bell is a content journalist currently studying a Creative Writing MA. She has been writing since she was five years old, penning tales of pirates for her long-suffering family to read. Libraries and lattes are her life.

Luca Serra

Luca Serra is a third-year BA Illustration Animation student at Kingston University. Fluidity is the keyword that characterises his practice, whether that's through the mediums, subjects, or forms of his work. He aims to produce effeminate and androgynous imagery which blurs the line across the gender binary and captures exuberant and sexual energy.

Xyvah M. Okoye

Xyvah M. Okoye is a reader, writer, and part-time human. She writes stories about gods, monsters, and damaged royals who petition them.

Deborah Thompson

Deborah Thompson is a Creative Writing MA student at Kingston University, as well as a Graphic Designer, a Pilates teacher, and a mother of two teenagers. She is most interested in writing short stories and flash fiction, and has had a couple of flash stories published online by Myslexia and Flash Fiction Magazine.

Phoebe Levins

Phoebe is a queer, autistic person. She writes poetry that explores queer love and the intensity of those feelings whilst also enjoying writing horror prose and watching horror movies. Phoebe enjoys exploring themes of trauma and religion in their horror writing and often writes Southern Gothic horror – a genre with limited content available. She is also passionate about autistic and queer acceptance.

Saleha Bakhtiar

Saleha Bakhtiar is a part-time artist and MPharm student who enjoys philosophical poetry and debate. She has only recently begun to promote her artwork, with "Two Horns" displaying ideas of struggle that lead to self-awareness and self-revolution.

Ruairidh MacLean

Ruairidh MacLean is a Creative Writing (Distance Learning) MA student at Kingston University. He is a South Londoner, of mixed Scottish and Afro-Caribbean heritage. He taught

English Language in Croydon for six years but gave that up to pursue a lifelong desire in fiction writing. He has a few cultural articles published under the name Caliban's Revenge.

About Kingston University Press

Kingston University Press has been publishing high-quality commercial and academic titles since 2009. Our list has always reflected the diverse nature of the student and academic bodies at the university in ways that are designed to impact on debate, to hear new voices, to generate mutual understanding and to complement the values to which the university is committed.

While keeping true to our original mission, and maintaining our wide-ranging backlist titles, our most recent publishing focuses on bringing to the fore voices past and present that reflect and appeal to our community at the university as well as the wider reading community of readers and writers in Kingston, the UK and beyond. As well as publishing the work of writers and poets from the university's vibrant writing community, we also partner with other disciplines around the university, and organisations from our local community, to bring their content to a wider readership, and publish our own editions of older works.

Our books are all edited, designed and produced by students on Kingston University's MA and BA Publishing courses, whose creativity and publishing skills bring the projects to life.

Follow us on Twitter **@KU_press** and Instagram **@kingstonuniversitypress**